The things they never tell you about becoming mum

The things they never tell you about becoming mum

Sharon Smyth

To order additional copies of this book, contact:
Xlibris Corporation
0-800-644-6988
www.xlibrispublishing.co.uk
Orders@xlibrispublishing.co.uk
304718

Contents

Acknowledgements

Huge gratitude to my new parent friends whose support, humour, and shoulders to cry on were truly a godsend. Thank you especially to those of you, you know who you are, who kindly read my book and gave me your views and encouragement.

This book is dedicated to my beautiful baby girl – Ellie. Words simply cannot express the wonder and joy you bring.

Hello . . .

. . . my name's Sharon. When I turned thirty-one, I gave birth to one amazing daughter, who, as I write this, is now almost three. I'm not special in any particular way nor am I particularly different from hundreds of other mums out there, so why I have written this book?

Well, for a variety of reasons, I decided to write down my experiences of becoming a mum, and my friends and family encouraged this crazy idea. Writing things down made me feel good and, especially early on, helped me to keep a sense of me – the me that wasn't just about having a baby and coping, the me that had been a career-driven woman, the me that liked order and predictability, and the me that liked to be in control.

This last key fact will be very relevant in several places in the forthcoming pages where I refer to myself, in a positive sense, as a control freak. I like to be in control of my life as much as possible, meaning that I like to plan ahead, know what's happening, and feel that I can influence it. I don't think this is unusual, but it is challenging within the context of having a baby.

So why should you read this?

This isn't a scientific fact-filled book and nor is it designed as a guide to parenthood. I am not, and do not pretend to be, an expert on any of this. I have one amazing baby girl who was only twelve weeks old as I started to write this. Of course, she will be considerably older by the time I finish it as it has to be written in short chunks when she allows me time, and I mean short chunks – five minutes was good going to start with!

This book was my way of keeping my sanity and recording for others some of the things that nearly drove me mad or made me howl with laughter.

Here then are the things I wish someone had told me, given in what I hope is a logical order, starting with items relevant to pregnancy. I hope you find this a helpful read and, most of all, I hope it makes you laugh!

Sharon

Congratulations – You're Pregnant!

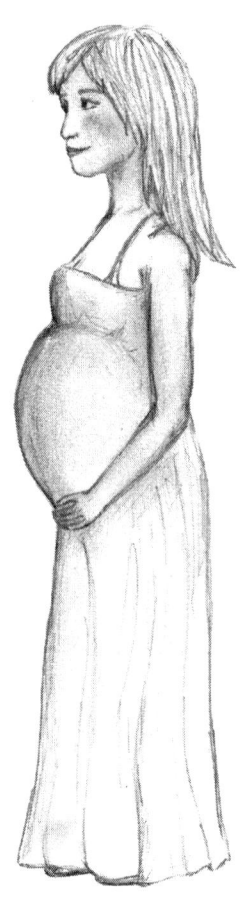

First, before we get started, I have to confess that I am one of those annoying people who actually, on the whole, loved my pregnancy. It should be noted that, like most pregnant ladies, I did endure my share of uncomfortable side effects: morning sickness (the highlight of which was throwing up in a work friend's car before I had even told her I was pregnant!), heartburn, a really, really huge belly, and the most horrifically itchy belly (more on that later). Despite this, I do tend to err on the glass-half-full philosophy of life and hence these unfortunate side effects didn't make, and haven't made, me feel any less positive about my pregnancy.

Similarly, I feel lucky for the way my labour and birth went. No, I didn't cough and, hey presto, produce a baby, and no, it's not an experience I want to repeat every day, but I feel positive about how it went. This is what makes me feel lucky.

Second, it goes without saying that everyone's pregnancy, labour, and birth of their baby is different; it's a very personal experience. That said, there are some things which I think are sound points for all.

These two things mean that my writing on this particular topic will not be an endless list of potential problems, a trip through medical terms, or a guide to the nine months. Instead, I will share with you the seven things which I wish someone had told me when I was pregnant – suffices to say, a list of seven seems like a reasonable number for women who are already coping with being pregnant.

1

Learn to zone out of unhelpful conversations

For some reason, once you are pregnant, everyone will feel it is acceptable, even required, to give advice and share their stories. Always (yes, always) switch off at these points in the conversation and concentrate instead on the little one growing inside your belly. Positive thinking is the only way to go when it comes to your birth and labour – fact.

Don't get me wrong. I *love* talking about my pregnancy; it was an amazing experience, and I love to share it, but I share when asked, when someone looks interested, and I share carefully. Unfortunately, this is something which, it appears, ninety-nine per cent of the population are unable to do.

The most appalling example of this is that everyone (including complete strangers) will now feel compelled to share with you their birth horror stories. I recall so many people revelling in seeing my reaction as they described their traumatic experience in detail. I was worried enough about how this whole birth thing was going to work as it was!

There are, of course, several other situations in which you should always zone out:

- 'Enjoy your pregnancy, and get lots of rest now while you can.' This is one of the most common pieces of advice given when people first find out that you are expecting, and to my mind, it is also totally unhelpful. Not every aspect of pregnancy is enjoyable, and being told to enjoy it will not make you do so!

- 'Don't worry, dear. The nightly toilet trips are good practice for when your little one arrives – its nature's way.' The truth here is that the several nightly trips to the loo, which you are no doubt making at stages in your pregnancy, are really horrific breaks in sleep. So let's give a big thanks to Mother Nature since we now effectively suffer disturbed sleep in advance too! Add to that the fact that the kindly souls sharing this advice with me always appeared to be taking great enjoyment out of effectively saying I would get less rest when my bundle arrived. Even if this is true, is it too much to ask that people don't wish it on us with such gusto?

2

Plan the birth!

I know it sounds ridiculous and don't get me wrong, I'm not suggesting that you can select exactly what type of birth you want and hey presto, that is what you get. This is about doing your research now so that you understand what does and could happen during labour and birth as well as the options and choices you have. Knowing your preferences for different eventualities, understanding the local healthcare options and being clear with your birth partner and midwife about them can be incredibly reassuring. But . . . prepare also for the fact that any and all plans or ideas you have may go out of the window when the day arrives – you may change your mind, or circumstances may make your original plans impossible. In the end, the resulting little one is all that matters.

Crucially, remember to talk to your birthing partner about the whole labour and birth process. Whether your partner, other family member, or friend is coming along, they too need to be prepared. If it's their first birth, then they will also be concerned about how they will cope and what they should do; discussing it makes it easier for them to support you better.

My husband and I agreed in advance that his role was to:

- Be there physically as support – well, he was definitely partly to blame for this state of affairs, so he can lose sleep and watch at least! In fact, when the midwife told me for the third time that I wasn't in labour, despite my contractions, I finally decided that I didn't care – I wouldn't be sleeping, so neither would he. I promptly demanded he come into the hospital immediately to join me, even if I wasn't in real labour! But it turns out I was, and after four hours, our daughter arrived. Ha, take that midwife!

- Act as my advocate (making sure we were involved in any decisions and providing me with a sanity check) and ensure that I knew exactly what was going on in terms of the medical help, the process of labour, and so on at all times. I knew that I would cope better with labour if I felt in control – not something easily achieved with this particular experience in life, but herein lay his challenge! For me, on the day this was a fantastic thing to do, and my inner control freak was aided both by my husband and a midwife, who quickly realised the more I knew, the better. She even took time to explain to me why, during the pushing phase, I could feel my daughter coming out and then going back in! (FYI – the aforementioned is absolutely normal and doesn't mean that you're not making progress.)

- Massage my back if I wanted – as it turns out, I couldn't stand it, and all he got for his trouble was a bellow of 'get off'!

Even with all this agreed, however, we couldn't foresee how he would feel when my daughter and I were rushed off after the birth. I truly believe that the process of birth, whilst incredibly emotional and physically demanding on me, was equally difficult for him (don't snort at me!). He had absolutely no control and no understanding of what I was thinking or feeling nor could he take away the labour process.

When my daughter and I both disappeared, he was left completely alone, in a delivery room, with all the emotions of amazement at the birth and our new daughter, fear for our daughter's health, worry for me, and, he would admit, shock at the whole thing. On the other hand, I was put totally at ease and relaxed whilst having some minor surgery, during which I grabbed a nap! (More on that later.)

3

Be positive but realistic about the birth

This is about ensuring you stay positive about your impending labour and birth, reminding yourself that your body is designed to do this and that it truly is amazing. Positive thinking is the only way to go. That said, at the same time, you need to be realistic. Labour and birth are not something which women would choose to do every day, and going into it thinking that it will be a breeze with no discomfort or difficulty is completely unrealistic. You are about to put your body through something truly dramatic, and you will feel it.

I should add that I have chosen not to use the word 'pain' at any point here. This is not because I am saying you won't think it painful, but simply because, as a word, it is far too broad a term and subjective. Needless to say, you will feel your labour and birth, and unless you are incredibly lucky, it won't all be nice feelings which you would choose to experience regularly. Ultimately, though, this is an amazing and natural thing – you can do it! If I'm honest, I simply could not get my head around how a baby would actually fit coming out, and even now, I have to say that it still amazes me that it is possible. But there's the point – it is possible; keep telling yourself that, by and large, Mother Nature is incredibly clever, and this does work.

This seems an appropriate place to add in a word or two about Caesarean births. The idea of having a Caesarean can, for many women, fill them with fear. These feelings are normal, and I was no different. A Caesarean was something I really hoped to avoid because an operation was scary, because I wasn't sure how I would care for my newborn afterwards, and because, if I am honest, I had this ideal view of wanting to experience labour and birth. I did feel that I should try to get my head around it, just in case – then, at least, I would understand the process so to speak. Ultimately, if it was necessary for the safety of the baby or me, then there was no doubt about what we would do, and this became my mantra when thinking about it.

As a final note on this particular subject, there are several things which a number of ladies I know who had Caesarean births strongly recommend women think about beforehand, just in case:

- Whatever the situation, you should expect hospital staff to talk you through what is happening and why. Ask questions.

- As with any type of birth, you still have some decisions to make, so it is worth including this in your birth plan, even when it is a planned Caesarean. Who will be with you? What does hospital policy allow them to see? What do they want to see? How will you find out the sex of the baby? Do you want to try to breastfeed in the theatre, in recovery, or not at all?

- Finally, and most importantly, you will need to get and accept help afterwards whilst you go easy and heal. Your body will need time.

4

Imagine what life with your newborn is going to be like . . . then get a reality check

In thinking about what life will be like with your new baby, prepare yourself for the fact that every baby is different. To cut to the chase, you've no idea how it's going to work and what it's going to be like.

Do not assume that your baby will arrive in the shape of a sleepy baby who sleeps, eats, and well . . . poos. Some babies are like this for a few weeks, some a few months, and some . . . never. You may have a very alert and noisy baby from day one, a baby that needs entertaining and amusing from the start. Prepare yourself for this and then, if this is your baby, it won't leave you too shell shocked but, hopefully, allow you to enjoy it – or at least cope with the onslaught of the first few weeks.

By all means, pray for a sleepy, happy-go-lucky baby, but prepare for another sort!

In my case, part of me hadn't allowed myself to think too far ahead for fear of tempting fate, and part of me lived in a world of sleepy babies. In reality, saying this may not make any difference, but at least someone has said it to you. Would I have believed someone who described how it might be? Probably not, and here's the rub – how can you get your reality check? None of the books I read did it for me. The child birthing classes I attended were great but didn't give me the reality check. Talking to people you know who have children older than six months is also unlikely to do it as they've usually forgotten.

So what can you do? I can think of just three things that might, just might, have helped me prepare:

- Number one: Take my word for it, newborn babies are hard work – you will be tired, you will have moments where you don't think you'll ever be yourself again, and you will wonder what on earth you did. More on this later, but it suffices to say, I wish someone had said this to me.

- Number two: Spend some real time with someone who's had a baby recently. I mean real time – not one hour or even half a day, and you also have to make sure it's someone who will be absolutely honest with you.

- Number three: Keep reading this book because it's not like other books, and maybe just hearing about how it was for me and my new parent friends will make it real to you.

My final words on this topic are two warnings. First, remember that your baby and your experience will be unique. Second, that having shared this 'wish someone had told me' with you, it still might not make any difference, but if you're just slightly less shocked than I was, then that's great.

5

Learn to be flexible now

This is all about preventing yourself from setting unrealistic expectations, so start right now by agreeing with yourself and your partner that you will both:

- Forget any set ideas you have in your head before you give yourself a headache that you don't need in addition to one inevitably caused by your crying newborn.

- Refrain from using statements such as 'I'll never give my baby a dummy' or 'I don't believe in young children watching TV', and instead, try 'I'd like it if . . .'

- Agree that your first goal is to survive the arrival of your beautiful newborn into your lives. Agree now that, for the first twelve weeks, you will not worry about whether what you are doing is 'storing up problems for the future' or whether it is in the book of 'perfect parenting' (the latter does not exist).

6

Get some friends

It may sound ridiculous, but finding some friends who are expecting little ones at around the same time as you is something that I truly believe every parent-to-be should do. Attending antenatal classes, an aqua natal group, or using some of the mum-to-be networking sites are all great ways of linking up with others, who will be an essential source of support in the months to come.

I simply cannot emphasise enough how important this is, and doing it beforehand means you can support each other during pregnancy and in the first few dramatic weeks. My friends were, and still are, a godsend.

A note of warning, though: only if you are open and honest about how you feel will others be the same, otherwise, it is pointless. You use more energy pretending everything is fine all the time than dealing with the challenges of a newborn.

7

You don't need to suffer with an itchy belly!

This is my final pregnancy related entry and will not be relevant to all, not even to the majority, but I simply had to include it. For those for whom this does become relevant, well, I hope this entry comes in handy . . .

During the last few weeks of pregnancy, the skin on your belly can stretch so much that it becomes sore and itchy. In my final two weeks, which took me to my forty-second (yes forty-second) week of pregnancy, my belly became a red beacon of itchiness which prevented me sleeping and got worse and worse. GP and midwife advice had been cold flannels and aqueous cream, with the GP not keen to prescribe steroid creams so late in pregnancy.

Finally, the day for me to be induced arrived, and I went into hospital. In the hot ward, I quickly settled down and unveiled my red belly to the air in an attempt to ease the need to scratch as if I had fleas. The very sweet midwife immediately gasped and exclaimed 'oh dear!' After realising that she was referring to the red soreness and not just the size of my huge belly, I explained that it had been like that for a couple of weeks. Rushing off, she quickly returned and suddenly lathered my belly in a creamy substance. The relief was instant and the secret answer – calamine lotion.

There is some humour in there somewhere about the irony of how easy the problem was to solve yet how impossible it had seemed at 1, 2, and 3 a.m. each night.

I should add that, several months on, I am still unable to see the humour or irony.

The message is simple: try calamine lotion.

8

How to *really* write a birth plan

When I first wrote this book, I only included the bullet points from the previous chapter regarding our birth plan. However, when one of my friends read this, she asked me why I wasn't including my whole plan. She promptly reminded me about how we all talked about birth plans within our group but really struggled with where to start in practice. For this reason, here is my entire birth plan, exactly as originally written. I hope it is both interesting and helpful in starting your own.

It's worth saying at this point that, as suggested earlier, it is unlikely you will follow your plan exactly, and I didn't. When the time came, there were some things I wasn't able to do, such as starting my labour at home, and some things I, in the end, didn't want to do. This included using the TENS machine (which was, for me, just an annoyance) or having music in the delivery room (it really didn't cross my mind). I did, however, find the birth plan incredibly helpful; we felt informed and prepared, hospital staff read it as each shift started, and in the main, we were able to stick to all the key things like being mobile and helping me to feel in control.

Our 'ideal' birth plan focuses on low intervention, natural, active birth using good positioning, breathing, and relaxation. This birth plan is not meant to be rigid. We are happy to change it, after discussion with you, if there are problems with Sharon's labour.

Sharon is a 'control freak' and would like to be kept informed of labour progress and what is happening at all times.

Labour/birth partner

Husband – present throughout the labour and birth, supporting with breathing, positions, and keeping Sharon informed!

Pain relief

- Use of yoga breathing and positions using a yoga ball.
- Walking and moving around.
- Use of TENS machine (starting at home).
- Relaxation in bath (with labour bubble bath).
- Sharon may want to use gas and air to supplement the above.
- Music in delivery room (in labour bag).
- Massage by husband (with labour massage oil).

Pethidine – if necessary. Ideally a reduced dose to enable Sharon to still feel in control. (Husband should check at that time that it is not too late to have this so that it does not affect the baby.)

Epidural – to be avoided if at all possible.

If labour slows down, Sharon would like to try some different positions to get things moving again before other interventions are tried.

Artificial rupture of membrane to be avoided if at all possible.

Forceps and ventouse – to be avoided if at all possible. If required, preference for ventouse rather than forceps.

If a Caesarean is necessary for the health and wellbeing of Sharon or the baby:

- Husband to be present in the theatre during Caesarean, if possible.
- Ideally, Sharon wants to be awake for the procedure.
- Skin-to-skin contact with Sharon immediately after delivery. If not possible, skin-to-skin contact with husband.
- Sharon does not want to breastfeed in the theatre but would like to try, if she is able to do so herself, when in recovery.

Monitoring:

Sharon prefers intermittent monitoring to enable her to remain mobile.

Delivery:

- Preference for upright positions such as leaning against the bed or wall or on all fours, with a leg stretched forward.
- If a lying down position is required, or if Sharon gets tired, Sharon wants to be on her side, with her right leg supported by husband or the midwife.
- Sharon would like to be able to feel the head when it crowns.
- Husband does not want to cut the cord – but please check at that time!

Immediately after delivery:

- We would like the baby to be given straight to us after the birth for skin-to-skin contact with Sharon or, if this is not possible, skin-to-skin contact with daddy.
- We would like to find out the sex of our baby ourselves.
- Vitamin K injection to be administered to our baby.

Third stage:

- Sharon would like the syntocinon injection to speed up the third stage but would like to wait five to ten minutes before the cord is clamped and the injection given.
- Assuming all is well, after the birth, we would like some quiet time with our new baby on our own in the delivery room.
- Sharon would like to breastfeed as soon as she is able after the birth and would only like assistance if she asks for it.

9

The real story about birth

This chapter is simply my daughter's birth story. It's included in this book to offer a real-life take on birth that isn't set to scare, deceive, or influence you in any way. It isn't gory, over-the-top, or full of horror – just a record of how it was for us exactly as I wrote it just a few weeks after the event.

This is included because I simply couldn't find birth stories that were literally just that – a story about what happened and how it felt. They were all dramatic or focused on a particular aspect or, worse still, tried to influence my choices. I share this in the hope that those of you who choose to read it find this an interesting read.

On your mark . . .

8.30 a.m. 30 March. Arrive at hospital: I was forty-two weeks pregnant, and despite having a membrane sweep and trying all the traditional old wives' tales (curry, pineapple, scrubbing floors, sex (yes really!), walking etc.), I had to go to the hospital to be induced.

It felt very strange because we were going into hospital whilst I wasn't in labour at all, but we duly arrived at Ipswich Hospital at the required time. I was disappointed at having to be induced which meant I could neither be on the midwife-led ward as I had hoped nor be at home for the early stages of labour. Alas, my dramatic dash to, and entrance into, the hospital was not to be.

My husband and I were both very nervous because everyone, and everything you read, seemed to suggest that induced labour could be more painful than non-induced labour, and if we needed the drip, contractions could come on very strongly, very quickly. To top it off, we also knew that it still might not work and might result in a Caesarean section. This was something we were hoping to avoid partly on the basis that I was worried about undergoing an operation for the first time and mostly because I was concerned about the much longer time it would take for me to heal and be up and about.

We went straight up to the ward and were shown to a room of four beds. We were introduced to our midwife for the shift, and I was put on a heart monitor to check the baby's heart beat and any contractions.

10 a.m. After an hour of monitoring, I was given a prostaglandin pessary to soften the cervix and, hopefully, start inducing labour. I had to lie still and be monitored for another twenty minutes after which time I could get up. As soon as the twenty minutes were done, we decided to go for a walk. I could feel period-like pains, and walking helped take my mind off it, plus we knew that staying up and active was good for encouraging labour. The plan was for the next pessary to be put in after six hours, unless labour started before. We spent six hours walking around and around the hospital grounds and going to the café for drink and food.

3 p.m. We were back in the ward, and I was being monitored again before the next pessary could be put in. I was still feeling what seemed like period pains to me, and the machine showed 'tightenings', although the midwife explained that this wasn't really labour because I wasn't dilated at all.

4 p.m. Second pessary was put in and after another twenty minutes of monitoring, confirming the baby's heartbeat was normal and that the tightenings were stronger; it was time to go walking around again! The walking really helped, partly because it gave us something to do instead of simply waiting and partly because I truly believe it encouraged my labour. There was the unfortunate side effect of blisters on my feet, which took weeks to heal! (A helpful friend has since asked me why I didn't wear backless shoes – so something to think about for others there!)

7 p.m. Eventually, in the early evening, we went back to the ward and tried to relax a little.

Get Set . . .

11 p.m. With the pains still strong, the midwife confirmed that I still wasn't dilating and advised that my husband go home and that I get some sleep! To enable me to get some of the recommended sleep, I was offered either a sleeping tablet or a pethedine injection. I opted to have a small dose of pethedine on the basis that we knew it would be a big day tomorrow, and, to be fair, I didn't think a sleeping tablet was going to do much!

11.20 p.m. Unfortunately, twenty minutes later, the tightenings weren't any weaker, so I spoke to the midwife, who again sweetly said I should just try to get some sleep! It felt strange for both me and my husband. I felt as I'd expected to feel when in labour, but I wasn't really, and my husband felt odd leaving me to go home.

Nonetheless, he went home, and I spent the next couple of hours walking around the ward on my own – sleep was not an option with the discomfort I was in.

The time was taken up with my walking around the ward, pausing for short moments when the tightenings came on, and periodically trying to sit or lie down on the bed, which I quickly realised was extremely uncomfortable. This felt like labour to me.

And we are off . . .

1 a.m. I sat back on the bed, resting for a minute from walking around, and my waters suddenly broke. I didn't particularly feel anything at all. I just felt the water and realised I was soaked (much more than I had imagined!). I called the midwife to help me clear up the mess and get changed and phoned my husband to tell him the news. The midwife advised that this still didn't necessarily mean anything immediately, so there was no need for my husband to come back in yet.

1.10 a.m. After walking around the ward for another ten minutes, I decided that, quite frankly, this was too uncomfortable, and the tightenings were so strong now that even if I wasn't in labour, my husband could just get back to the Hospital anyway! I spoke to the midwife, who said that he could come back in if that's what I wanted and that she would move me to a delivery room. I got the distinct impression that she didn't think anything was really moving yet and that I was being a bit melodramatic! Moi?

I phoned my husband and couldn't even talk through the contractions now (note: I am officially calling them contractions at this stage), but I managed to ask him to come back in. My husband asked if I had tried any gas and air, which I had completely forgotten about! I quickly asked for this and was moved to a delivery room.

Whilst my husband came back to the hospital, I opted to have another small dose of pethedine. Before administering the injection, the midwife examined me and found that I was four centimetres dilated. I was truly overjoyed that finally things were moving and the contractions did actually mean something.

2 a.m. My husband arrived back at the ward, and I remember giving him this huge beaming smile and saying, 'I'm four centimetres'. He has since told me that I repeated this news several times to him because I was so excited!

It was at this point that I shouted to get me an epidural because it was all too bloody painful, so my husband went to ask the midwife, who had popped out. Having read my birth plan, the midwife told him that 'she doesn't really want one' and convinced him to get me to wait thirty minutes and see if I still wanted one then. He very bravely told me this and, in what must have been a gap between contractions, I said fine. In the end, I didn't have an epidural for the labour or birth.

2.30 a.m. From then on, things really started moving (hence the diary includes few specific times from here until the birth itself!). Contractions were coming every few minutes and with them an overriding urge to push.

Unfortunately, as I wasn't fully dilated, I wasn't supposed to push. The midwife explained that pushing too early would cause me to bruise and swell, delaying the birth or possibly even preventing a normal delivery. The urge to push was, however, totally overwhelming and continued for the rest of the labour – four and a half hours until I could actually push! I later found out that this was unusual but likely to be caused by the position of the baby. On the positive side – this gave me something to focus on.

Once again, the pethedine I had been given appeared to have no effect; however, the gas and air was amazing. It took the edge off each contraction and gave me something to do other than push. In addition, to distract from pushing, I talked to my husband when I could, used the birthing ball to rock and bounce, panted during contractions, and ran, skipped, or jumped around the delivery room. Yes, literally.

As per our birth plan, I stayed mobile and upright throughout the labour, and the midwife respected this at all times. She checked my heart rate and the baby's heart rate intermittently by crawling on the floor or kneeling down to reach!

It was at some point during this time that I decided I was too hot and stripped off down to my bra. It felt great – though I must have looked hideous and, I should imagine, quite amusing when skipping around the room!

During the labour, I remember having various conversations, including one about how we still didn't have a boy's name agreed on and lots about the gas and air and not overdoing it. In total, I did manage to polish off four full canisters, which I now understand is fairly heavy going. I also remember snapping, when my husband was reminding me not to push, that I 'just can't help it – there is nothing I can do'!

I'm reliably informed that we had several conversations that I don't remember. At one point, I said that I was worried that the people waiting outside couldn't have the room yet as I wasn't finished. Apparently, I was reassured that no one was waiting for the room. And at one point, I was also very worried that there wasn't enough parking at our house for all the visitors!

The closing straight, the finishing line is in sight . . .

6.30 a.m. At last, the midwife said she could see the head, and I could start to push. I remember the discomfort I felt when I pushed and saying 'I don't want to' – to which I clearly remember the midwife smiling and saying something about there being no pleasing me, 'first you want to push when you can't and then you don't want to when you can!' She was right of course.

The contractions slowed down at this stage, being much more spaced out.

The midwife reassured us that this was normal to allow the baby and me to adjust. It was really strange because, in between contractions, I felt totally normal and could have full, sane conversations. I had also stopped using gas and air by now and was just using my breathing.

With each contraction, the midwife asked me to push as hard as I could; it felt like I was squeezing a melon out, and yes, that was uncomfortable! At one stage, I described how I could feel the baby moving down as I pushed but then going back up again once the contraction stopped. The midwife explained that this was fine and that it was good, gradual progress, and this was normal. Normal but annoying.

At one stage, I remember asking the midwife how much longer this would take, and she said 'the pinny is coming on now, so that's a good sign' and promptly put a full-length, plastic pinny on! Finally, the head began to crown, and as per our birth plan, the midwife told me so that I could put my hand down to feel the head being born. The head felt tiny, warm, and soft. It was at this stage that the midwife asked me to pant a little to slow things down and prevent too much tearing.

The midwife also told my husband that now was the time if he wanted to look. Prior to the time, he hadn't been sure he wanted to look but was fascinated when it came to the crunch. Picture it – I was wearing just a bra, stood up with my hands bracing against the bed, leaning forward. My husband and the midwife behind me, kneeling down to see. I clearly recall them discussing what was happening behind me. Lovely.

7 a.m. Just thirty minutes after the head could first be seen, Ellie was born, just one big push after the head was out. It was an enormous relief to feel her finally come out, which she did with quite a gush of fluid and blood. (Now you know what the pinny is for.) My husband watched as she came out and saw the midwife quickly unravel the cord from around her neck.

Ellie was lifted straight up in-between my legs from behind me into my hands so that I could hold and see her. I lifted my leg over the cord, not one of my most elegant moments, but to be fair, elegance was not my top priority. I remember just staring at her. She was breathing but was very grey and gasping for her first breaths. I looked to see if it was a girl or a boy and looked up across the bed at my husband, yelling, 'it's a girl!'

The midwife then cut and clamped the cord, and the second midwife, who was present for the very last part, took Ellie to the resuscitation table to give her some oxygen to help her breathing. Whilst Ellie was having oxygen, I started to deliver the placenta. I don't remember having the injection to speed up the placenta delivery, but I did. I remember this bit being really uncomfortable.

And we are done . . .

Whilst I was still delivering the placenta, Ellie was brought back over to us and laid on my chest. I remember looking at her and lifting her head to my breast to see if she would feed, but she didn't. The midwives decided that she was a bit too floppy and drowsy and explained that they were going to call for a paediatrician to have a look at Ellie. They were very calm and didn't seem worried.

Once the placenta was out, the midwife looked at my tearing to see if she could sew it. Unfortunately, I had torn some muscle (third-degree tears), so I had to be stitched in the theatre.

I was rushed off in one direction, and at the same time, it was also decided that Ellie needed some help, so she was taken away too.

I was given a spinal (pain relief injected into the spine to numb you from the waist down) and stitched up in theatre whilst Ellie was taken to special care. I particularly remember the really nice man who collected me from the delivery room and wheeled me down to the pre-op room. He then took me into the theatre and stayed with me whilst I had the spinal. Most of all, I remember him saying that they would 'keep me covered up' until the surgeon arrived – I also remember snorting at him and saying that it wasn't an issue as I had lost all dignity several hours ago.

In the theatre, I was very calm, not really realising that Ellie was so poorly. I had the spinal and then a little nap whilst they operated.

Once done, I went into a recovery room for a few minutes before being wheeled up to my ward where my husband was waiting. When I saw him in the ward and not my daughter, I was confused at first and then panicked about where she was.

I recall being wheeled into the ward in my bed and seeing him sitting there looking positively grey. On asking him how Ellie was, he simply burst into tears. I remember holding his hand and asking him to nod if she was OK. He did and then I just reassured him and kissed his hand whilst I waited until he could explain. There was thirty seconds in there where I thought the worst, but with his nod, my main emotion became one of pain for the agony he had gone through. He had watched as we were both wheeled off, seen Ellie surrounded by medical staff whilst getting emergency attention, and been alone, fearing for Ellie.

Whilst I had been in the theatre, my husband had gone to special care to see Ellie when she was being treated – he has since described this as 'truly overwhelming', with lots of people leaning over and doing things to our tiny baby. He also recalls how one of the senior staff took him to one side to explain what was happening and, realising he wasn't taking it all in, patiently explained again, as well as writing it down for him. Ellie was getting help as she had fluid in her lungs and had swallowed a lot of rubbish - blood, amniotic fluid, and meconium (her first poo).

At this point in the story, I must make one specific editorial point and squeeze in number ten on my list of things I wish someone had told ~~me~~ us. **Number 10: Never forget how emotional this time is for your partner** as well. In the immediate time after the birth, my husband's emotions were as raw and dramatic as mine.

I was finally able to go up and see Ellie once I had some feeling back in my legs and body from the waist down – a frustrating wait. I remember the nurse asking me if I wanted to hold Ellie and then carefully getting her out of the incubator for me. This was the first time I held her after the birth, a brief and surreal moment.

So that's it, the end of our birth story and the beginning of our new family. It was an amazing life-changing experience which, all in all, I feel extremely positive about and lucky to have had. This leaves me just one last thing to say. Our family will be forever grateful for the amazing care that Ellie and I received at Ipswich Hospital, both in the labour ward and in special care.

The staff were truly fantastic. Thank you.

10

Welcome to the amazing world of newborns – brace yourself!

It has finally happened. After nine months of waiting (more if you've been trying for a while beforehand), you have finally made it through; the waiting is over, and your beautiful newborn is here. You've joined the club of parenting. You now have the right to talk incessantly about how well your little one is doing, how much milk they are drinking, how many poos and what consistency they produce, and, of course, how much sleep they and everyone else in the household is getting. Huge congratulations.

Now, first things first – everything you are feeling is normal, and everyone (no, really, everyone!) feels like they have no idea what to do. Oh, hang on, most of us really don't know what to do!

You are now on probably the steepest learning curve you will ever have, and the helpful advice which everyone will give you of 'trust your instinct' and 'you'll find your own way, you know your baby' will not help. I remember hearing this advice from many people, including my midwife, and even to this day cannot understand it. I hadn't had a baby before; no one had taught me anything about looking after a newborn (except for washing her), and I didn't know this little person yet. I was clueless, and absolutely nothing could change that. As someone who (as you already know) likes to be in control, this was the first huge challenge I faced. It does get easier, and you do get to know your son or daughter, but it is not, for many, an immediate revelation – which is unfortunate since expectations are often that it should be.

Now that that's out in the open, let's move on. You will now be *very* busy, and time will be scarce. It is at this point that you will now fully understand why this book is written in really tiny bite-size chunks – you really can read this once your baby is here – and I hope that you find it worthwhile managing to do this one thing for yourself and taking a few minutes to read each bit.

Read on then, as here are the six things I simply *have* to share about having a newborn. There were so many other things I had noted down when I initially 'wrote for my sanity', but, on reflection, those included are the ones that really . . . well . . . I think (and yes, it's just my opinion, so make your own choice) you really should know and no one seems to tell you.

11

Now is the time to make the most of those new baby friends

You will recall earlier the suggestion I gave to 'get some new baby friends'. It was at this point, with my newborn baby girl, that the friends I had made via antenatal classes really made a difference; they had also very recently had their babies, and within my group, there was always at least one person who could specifically relate to any individual issue.

The following is an email trail between me and some of our little group from when my daughter was a week old. This was the first of many occasions when I felt utterly relieved to have other people who were experiencing the same thing, to talk to. Whilst my initial email may seem rather chirpy, at that time, I was stressed, sleep deprived, and desperate to find someone else who understood. (Please see my 'translation' in brackets.)

N.B. The emails below are not included to give advice on what to do but to show a) why your friends are so important and b) that everyone shares the same issues to start with.

Hi Guys,

At one week in and just three days at home, I now have complete admiration for how L, C, and K managed to bring their bundles of joy to mine the other week and look so relaxed! (I do not understand. How did you get to my house? How did you get dressed . . . you must have lied about being OK!)

As promised, finally, attached are two photos of Ellie.

Whilst I am emailing, I would be grateful to know if anyone else is finding breastfeeding painful on the nipples, and if so, what have you done that helps? (This is agony - I hate it. Why did no one else say it was like this - are you all finding it easy? It must be me.)

Also, Ellie is really difficult to settle to sleep. She really fights it and then gets overtired and v upset. Is anyone else having similar issues, and have you any useful tips? (She doesn't sleep, she just screams - constantly. Surely this is not normal?)

Any advice welcome! (Please, please help me.) Hope you are all well.
X

Reply 1:

Hello! She's beautiful! What a gorgeous little face.
Thought I'd copy everyone in, in case anyone also has some advice for me.

Researching breastfeeding problems and solutions is becoming a part-time job for me since I'm now four weeks in and still suffering from cracked and v sore nipples! Don't worry, this is not the norm!

The midwives have told me all along that he's latched on perfectly and feeding well, but it shouldn't be painful then. I eventually discovered that a) he has thrush in his mouth and in my breasts (just got correct medication this morning), b) he is slightly tongue-tied so can't feed hundred per cent correctly, and c) I have a fast let-down reflex, which means the milk spurts out very quickly, and to try to stem the flow, baby S squirms and clamps down on the nipple and bends it back.

You should definitely have the infant-feeding specialist midwife around if you haven't already. I'm sure there must be one for your area. They can double-check that Ellie's latched on properly, and they can also give you different positions to try. Have you tried the rugby ball position under the arm? Sometimes, it helps to vary the position and put pressure on a different part of the nipple. I'm sure you know this, but check that Ellie has a big mouthful of nipple and her bottom lip is bent backwards with her chin against the breast.

I found breastfeeding to be absolute agony for the first few weeks, and my nipples were bleeding! If it's very bad, you could use nipple shields which were the only thing that enabled me to carry on with it for a few days when it was really bad. I also express and feed from a bottle when it's very bad. I have an electric pump, borrowed from a friend, which is very good (and makes me feel like a dairy cow). Even with my various problems it did get a lot less painful after two weeks, so hang in there! I'm always happy to chat about your breastfeeding problems as I'm becoming quite obsessed with the subject as you can probably tell!

As for the sleep, have you tried swaddling her? Midwives don't recommend it these days due to overheating, but I know a lot of people (including C!) who swear by it. Baby S hated it with a passion and went nuts, so we haven't persevered with it, but I know of lots of babies who love it.

I suppose you've tried the usual rocking, carrying, etc. The pram should be good for getting her off to sleep, although baby S wakes up the second we come back into the house! I was very keen to get baby S used to settling himself in his own bed from day one, but after a few days with a screaming baby, I'll now do anything to get him to sleep when he's over-tired or has a tummy ache. He's often awake for five hours or more in the mornings with a tummy ache! I've found he likes to be in the sling and then I can put him in his cot once he's dosing off.

Good luck! Let me know how you get on. I hope everyone's well.
Love, L x

Reply 2:

Hi!

Thanks for copying in - really helpful! Two weeks in, and we're still trying to find our feet and constantly feel like I'm feeding all the time - sometimes hourly.

Would you believe he's lost weight too with all that guzzling.

We too are investing in an expressing machine to see how that goes. As for nipples, mine are sore but not during the feed itself. I've got lanisoh, when I remember to put some on. A friend has recommended a homeopathic cream, which I'm going to get my hands on. I too had a breastfeeding counsellor in the hospital, and the midwives have been good. I've been referred to a breast clinic too as I had a rusty-coloured discharge at the beginning, which I'm told can be normal.

As for sleep, baby B likes to wave arms & legs around and generally drops off during feeding – well, why wouldn't you if it's constant? He seems to be OK with semi-swaddling. He absolutely hates his Moses basket, but loves car and pram travel – that seems to work. Like you, L, anything for sleep at the moment.

I've never had quite such an out-of-body experience as this feels – am told it will get better!

Hope you're all OK – hope to see you soon! B Xx

Reply 3:

Hi Guys,

Nice to know I'm not the only one suffering from lack of sleep. Baby R was feeding every hour (sometimes less), wasn't sleeping for any decent length of time, and constantly wanted to be on the breast. Breastfeeding hasn't been painful, but the amount she was feeding wasn't allowing my milk to replenish properly and wasn't, therefore, giving her the calories she needed. She was constantly losing weight. This happened with older bro, so I knew the signs. I now top up the breastfeeding with two or three two-ounce formula feeds. I was amazed when, by day two of doing this, baby R slept for over three hours! It was the longest she had slept in one go. She is a changed baby, much happier, and so am I. No more bouts of weeping from both of us.

Feeling pretty much recovered from the C-section and look forward to driving again, not to mention go shopping myself for pink things. How about getting together sometime next week at my house?

Lots of love to everyone. Family A

Reply 4:

Hi A! Would be good to catch up and see the babies and find out how everyone's doing! Sounds like we are all having fun with feeding and suffering from lack of sleep.

Hope you are well. See you soon. Love, K x

12

It's OK to feel that way. Getting to grips with your pesky post-birth emotions

For whatever reason Mother Nature saw fit, alongside the shock of having your newborn and the process of finding out what to do with them, we also have to deal with an array of post-birth emotions. I can't speak for how everyone feels after the arrival of their newborn, but from chatting with my parent friends and health professionals, it is clear that everyone has raging post-birth hormones and emotions.

Unfortunately, the expectation from you and everyone else is that you will have an array of positive feelings (joy, relief, pride, and amazement), and although you might be a bit tired, you will feel blissful happiness as a new mother. However, it is not that simple. I remember, in those first few weeks, literally swinging between laughing with joy one moment and sobbing with tears a while later. This is normal and was not post-natal depression. It was what I like to call 'newbie shock' – an array of negative feelings, which I truly did not expect to feel nor believed I should feel. So to put the record straight, alongside the excitement, amazement, and joy, the following less-than-positive feelings really are all absolutely normal:

- *Guilt* – This can sneak up on you from all sorts of places. Perhaps because in the middle of the night in hospital you allow (or even ask) the midwife to take your crying baby away so you can get some rest. Perhaps because in the middle of the night, after seven days with little sleep, you are so exhausted that you can't help wondering why you had this baby. Or perhaps even because there is that first time when you leave your baby to cry for a minute or two before picking them up or when you no longer breastfeed (whether by choice or not). Welcome to parent guilt.

- *Panic* – I vividly remember the utter panic when I was finally going to spend my first night with Ellie next to me in the ward. This feeling was at least equal to the feeling of relief that my baby was going to be next to me for the first time. I also keenly remember a well of panic when we got home for the first time and I realised that we had a baby and had absolutely no idea what to do with her. I remember carrying her into the house, putting her in her Moses basket, and sitting down to watch her, all the time thinking that we had absolutely no idea what we were doing.

- *Anger* – I remember feeling angry that no one could tell me how to settle my crying baby and angry that I had no idea how. I was angry that she kept crying and wouldn't sleep and angry at the smiling faces of people telling me to 'enjoy every minute'. Anger is an emotion which people don't often associate with having a baby, but for me, there it was.

The key to dealing with these emotions is twofold:

Firstly, accept them, and do not feel guilty for any feelings you have. However, as simple as it sounds in theory, this is incredibly difficult in practice. I didn't really get this right until quite sometime after Ellie arrived, but the way I did eventually get to grips with it was to say out loud how I really felt, to my husband, my parent friends, and my midwife. I felt an immense pressure to say how wonderful and amazing having my newborn was – and whilst some of this pressure was no doubt of my own creation, there were also clearly expectations from others.

Secondly, find one 'amazing' moment to cherish. When you first see your baby, when they smile or coo for the first time, or when they wake up in the morning happy and settled – these are all the times when you will know why being a parent is amazing. Remember these times, and cherish the happiness you feel. Then try your hardest to replicate how that feels when they are crying, whingeing, not sleeping, and so on. They need to feel loved whatever they are doing, and you need to remember how you love them so much, even when you are exhausted and feel clueless.

13

Feel free to ignore the little pearls of wisdom that you are told (no, really, do)

As with every stage of having children, this stage is no exception, and everyone will now feel the need to offer some helpful advice. OK, so I'm cheating here a little bit because number 12 is essentially the same as number 1, 'Learn to zone out of unhelpful conversations', but it's just too important not to include again at this stage.

Unfortunately, as always, much of the advice you'll be given is unhelpful, pointless, and, quite frankly, annoying. In addition, as already mentioned, there could not be a worse time emotionally for you to be given unhelpful advice.

I cannot recall the number of times I almost ended up screaming at someone offering me this kind of advice, although usually I either managed to walk away or burst into tears!

Here, then, are some of the most frequently given bits of advice that you will hear and some brief notes on each, which I hope will help.

- 'Enjoy every moment – it goes so quickly.' This is the one piece of advice that literally everyone will give you when they hear that your little one has arrived. It is also one of the most ridiculous statements anyone can say to a parent of a newborn. Try your hardest not to snort at the kindly person giving you this advice; just smile back at them and then go on as before – surviving the onslaught of the first few weeks moving between elation and sheer terror.

- 'Sleep when the baby sleeps.' This fantastic piece of advice is really good for those who are blessed with babies who sleep well during the day and who do actually take the opportunity to sleep. Well done to them! For those whose sleepy baby appears to be an excuse to get some jobs around the house done – please stop. For those who do not have this opportunity at all, get and accept help. Warning: for those who are blessed with a sleepy baby – try not to be too smug; he or she will one day wake from his newborn dreamy state.

- 'Breastfeeding doesn't hurt if the baby is latched on correctly.' This is another gem that makes you feel totally unprepared and, at the point of attempting to breastfeed, completely incapable. For a lucky few, this statement may well be true. However, almost everyone I know had to get through an initial pain barrier with breastfeeding. The thing is, logically this makes sense. Your nipples have never been ravaged in this way before (no, really!) and every few hours, so isn't it bound to hurt initially?!
Try lansinoh cream, use nipple shields occasionally if it takes the edge off, and believe that it will eventually stop hurting, and you will love breastfeeding (if breastfeeding is for you).

Finally, you are allowed to cry about this; it is normal.

- 'Sleeping like a baby.' I now know that this is a completely ridiculous phrase unless you mean: restlessly, loudly, and, more often than not, lightly! Many (although, I have discovered, not all) babies are noisy during their sleep. Learning when to ignore this is crucial for your sanity and both your and their long-term ability to sleep at night.

- 'Oh, he's hungry, dear.' Remember, babies don't just cry for food. They cry for attention, when they are tired, when they are uncomfortable, and sometimes, yes, I really do believe it's true, they just cry, and you won't know why. Smile politely at those people who, on hearing your baby cry, say 'ah, he must need feeding' and then ignore them whilst you try to figure out why they are crying.

14

It's OK to look, but don't become obsessed with comparing your little one with everyone else's.

Is your baby ... smiling yet? Lifting his head yet? Blowing raspberries yet? Grabbing her toys yet?

The list of potential 'comparison' questions is endless and is, quite frankly, the scourge of new parents. Every baby is unique, so don't bother causing yourself stress by comparing. Your baby will reach their milestones in their own time and their own way. Please try to resist the pressure to worry about why someone else's little one is doing something when your angel isn't yet. Even more importantly, remember that parents forget, and anyone reflecting on things that happened more than twelve months ago is likely to be mistaken.

For example, the mother of a seven-year-old once told me that her little one was crawling at two months. Um – possibly?

Of course, if you're genuinely worried and can't get it out of your head, then ask someone who will know – midwife, health visitor, or maybe even your GP (or ask all of them to get a rounded view).

In the meantime, let me reassure you that all babies genuinely do develop differently and at different times. The main thing is to enjoy really watching them grow, and yes, I really did enjoy seeing how Ellie changed and developed.

15

Colic is horrible,
but you will get through it (honestly)

I could not have written about newborns without including at least a mention of the horror that is colic. I truly hope this is never relevant for you, but I include it just in case.

If your baby has colic, you will know. There is no mistaking the continuous screaming most commonly, though not always, from around 6 p.m. to midnight every night.

All babies cry; colicky babies scream and don't stop for hours. For those whose little ones don't have this, trust me, you can thank your lucky stars.

Colic is horrific not just because of the lost sleep or because of how sorry you feel for your little one or even because 'science', in the main, can't explain why they get it nor how to solve it but because it arrives when your hormones are still doing an almighty jig.

In experiencing a baby with colic, it is highly likely that you will have some, if not all, of the following thoughts. These are usually accompanied by crying, screaming, and shouting at your partner, who, importantly, will probably experience some similar thoughts though less hormone fuelled:

- Will they ever sleep? And will I?
- *?*! Why did I have a baby?
- This must be my fault. I'm a bad mother already.
- I simply cannot do this.
- My life is doomed.

Everyone, health professionals included, will repeatedly say 'it really will pass', 'just hang in there', and 'colic usually goes at three months'. I could reiterate all of these points, but this reassurance is as pointless as asking you to enjoy the crying. Instead, I will boldly offer some advice based on my personal experience:

- Look for any ways to help them reduce their wind and stomach pains, like using bottles that are anti-colic, trying baby massage and baby yoga, looking at how you can hold them most comfortably. Most of all, get help – a good baby yoga specialist or a colic nurse is a good place to start.

- Colic is often, though not always, linked to over stimulation; this opens up a whole world of other things you can do to help. Think about whether they are taking sufficient naps, about how to prevent too much stimulation, and about having fewer visitors etc.

- Contact all of your 'baby friends' and find out if anyone else is having a similar experience. It is a lifeline.

- Share the pressure and work with your partner, even if they are working in the day; you will need their help at night.

- Get out of the house. This may even help your little one immediately, but at the very least, it makes you feel human.

16

You can't avoid the new parent debates, and they really are emotional

As I write this, my daughter is now nine months old, and it has suddenly dawned on me that, so far, parenthood has involved a series of big questions or debates which our little family and our new parent friends have all been navigating and worrying about. Aside from the periodic lack of sleep and constant worrying about whether enough food is going in (and sufficient coming out), the 'debates' have been the other key sources of stress of new parenthood. It also strikes me that these are things which everyone faces, so why not introduce them all now and get them out of the way?

Of course, there is no point my suggesting that reading this will help you navigate these debates. It won't. I cannot provide answers. You will still have the debates, still obsess about some of them, and still feel as though you are guessing. This is normal and you will need to accept that there is no right or wrong answer. This section, then, is one purely for reassurance that this is normal and, hopefully, for a giggle!

Debate number one: breast or bottle?

This is the mother of all debates for new and expectant parents, and because, in reality, this one really gets going before your little one even appears, you are probably already mid-flow in it. Everyone has a view, and you are required to listen and agree with them all. Alongside this seems to be a view that everyone has a right to ask you whether or not you are breastfeeding and, demonstrated through the knowing looks afterwards, make a judgement on you.

My two favourite quotes on this particular debate have to be:

1. Health provider: 'So, do you intend to breastfeed or artificially feed your baby?' – and one wonders what they think is best?!

2. 'It's the best for your baby . . . everyone can do it.' – hmm, how very black and white. If only life didn't have shades of grey.

This is an incredibly emotive subject, and even now, on hearing this debate, I still feel the hairs on the back of my neck stand up. I simply will not offer advice on which way to go to anyone. How you choose to feed your baby is a very personal decision and something which may well change along the way. Making sure you are informed of the pros and cons and the pitfalls and issues from the start will help. So too will talking to other new mums, health professionals, and your partner, but, equally, try to remember that the bottom line is you want a happy, healthy baby.

I know mums who were simply unable to breastfeed for a variety of reasons, mums who chose not to breastfeed, mums who did mixed feeding (breast and bottle). And I also know mums who exclusively breastfed for timescales ranging from four to twelve months. The one thing they all had in common? They all, without exception, worried about whether what they were doing was the right thing and whether their baby was having enough milk, growing normally, and staying healthy.

If you aren't already discussing this, you will. It's normal, and spending hours talking about this subject alone is absolutely standard practice.

As an additional note, my other personal annoyance with this whole debate is that many people appear to have double standards. You feel a pressure to breastfeed but equally, in public, a pressure from people not to be anything other than absolutely discreet and, ideally, invisible when breastfeeding. Come on, make your mind up.

Debate number two: dummy or not?

Okay, the debate here goes something like this. On the plus side, having a dummy can help to settle a 'sucky' baby, and, according to many commentators, it can prevent thumb sucking, which is harder to stop later. It is also suggested that a dummy can help reduce the risk of Sudden Infant Death Syndrome (SIDS).

On the minus side, some people frown on dummies as ugly and unnecessary (that is, surely a baby can be settled in other ways?), and of course, there is always the future threat of how awful it is when a child still has a dummy when they are 'too old' for it.

I will not lie – this is a debate which, even now, I cannot resolve for myself.

Let's be clear. I am not a good example here of how to just make your own decisions and then get on with them.

My daughter had a dummy when she was in special care as a way of settling her when I had to leave, something a midwife very quietly suggested to us. Now, a year old, she still uses it for daytime naps and in the car when the journey becomes so unbearable because she simply has to whinge and shout constantly.

However, I still feel incredibly uncomfortable about it – there is no debate that she likes it and that it helps to relax her, but I don't like the way it looks (or how others look at her?), and I don't like the fact that she still needs it, albeit rarely.

This personal internal debate can, of course, become much worse when someone decides to weigh in on the issue. The most recent example of this was when I couldn't see Ellie, who was in the back carrier, and asked someone if she was OK, only to be told 'she's smiling, well, as much as you can see behind her dummy'. Thanks.

As a final note on this subject, I also know of several mums who wanted their baby to use a dummy, and actively encouraged them, only to find out that their little one didn't and wouldn't use it! Isn't life funny?

I just had to add a little further note in here. Ellie is now almost three-and-a-half (no idea how that happened). You may be interested to know that she hasn't had a dummy since she was eighteen months old, when the dummy fairy took it away and replaced it with a little gift because other babies now needed it as Ellie was too big!

Ellie does have two little cuddly toys that she always sleeps with and, if she wants them, takes them out with her. My key message here is that I'm not going to obsess about the teddies the same way I did about the dummy because it really was a huge waste of my energy.

Debate number three: routine versus baby-led (otherwise known as 'do you wake a sleeping baby?')

As with all these debates, there is no wrong or right answer here; what works for one doesn't necessarily work for another. Despite this, people get very sensitive about their choices on how to look after their little one (as I did too).

If I'm honest, this has been the one issue that has been able to cause more friction in new mum coffee times than any other.

My personal choice was to work towards a routine. I have friends who did similarly. I also know people who wanted to go with the flow more and see what their little one wanted to do. I have friends who did similarly. The point is that finding what suits you and your baby is a personal choice and depends upon your priorities.

So why did I choose a routine? Well, for several reasons:

- I always like to know what I am doing (or trying to do) and where we are. I wanted to plan my days – to know when I would need to feed so I could be somewhere convenient at that time and when she would need to sleep so I could be somewhere she could settle. The routine also helped me feel less clueless and acted as a kind of broad guide.

- Ellie was not a go-with-the-flow baby. She wasn't hungry one second but then screaming for milk the next. She was not tired and didn't want to sleep one minute, then screaming overtired the next. Ellie didn't show (and still often doesn't show) signs of tiredness; she went from awake to way overtired in a blink.

- I wanted to get a good night's sleep as soon as possible because I need my sleep, and I am horrid without it, but also because I believe that a good night's sleep is essential for Ellie's development. It is well-known that during our sleep we rest and recuperate, and dreaming helps us to process the events of the day. I believed a routine would help. Whilst, initially, this just meant having a 'bedtime' and keeping the very necessary night-time feeding quiet and sleepy, I believe that this set the tone for night-time. It also gave me some clear guidance around when to start stretching Ellie between feeds at night.

- Ellie had colic. A routine helped me cope and, I believe, in Ellie's case, helped with her colic because it prevented her becoming overtired.

Of course, a thought through routine has its disadvantages. I dared to wake a sleeping baby, and initially, it was genuinely hard work to get the routine up and going, and of course, if Ellie was ill, all bets were off. I also went through periods of being obsessive about the exact times of our routine.

So did Ellie sleep better, settle better, and feel happier because of the routine? I have absolutely no idea. I have no alternative against which to make a comparison. Sorry, folks, no answers here! Just please, please believe that there is no right or wrong, just what is right for you.

Debate number four: in their own room or in your room?

Current advice (at the time of having Ellie) is that your baby should sleep in your room for their first six months. Any suggestion that you might not follow this advice is generally met with frowns and looks of horror from health professionals and most others. The reasons for this advice appear to be that you can react quicker in an emergency, it's easier to feed your little one, and they need to make less fuss to get your attention, that is, they are less stressed.

We duly prepared a Moses basket and stand for our impending arrival and discussed where we might put it in our room. On getting home from the hospital, we set it all up on the first night and put Ellie down to sleep. It suffices to say that this is one of those things on which we quickly changed our minds, and on the second night home, Ellie was in her own room. Why? Because Ellie was a noisy and light sleeper, a deadly combination for sharing a room, especially with a mother who is quite literally crazy without sufficient sleep. It is fair to say that we disturbed Ellie as much as she disturbed us, and both sides were clearly unhappy with the arrangement, confirmed by Ellie's crying almost throughout the entire night.

On the second night, Ellie was in her own room, she slept much better, and so did I. But this is not the end of the story; on the third night, feeling guilty because of our decision and concerned that we 'should' have Ellie with us, we brought Ellie back into our room. In short – a disastrous decision where no one got any sleep at all. Night four, Ellie was back in her own room, where she stayed from then on!

I should just add that I always hear Ellie and quickly. Our monitor is a fairly standard one which clicks on whenever Ellie makes noise – shuffling, chatting, groaning, and, yes, crying. Pre-Ellie, I was a heavy sleeper, but this is no longer the case. I now often hear her from her room before the monitor clicks on.

My point, then, is this. Health professionals are required to advise in line with NHS guidelines, which are currently to have your baby with you at night. If I ever have a baby again, I have no doubt that I will try to follow this advice and have them in with me. However, this time, I wouldn't get so stressed if this really didn't work. In our situation, not sleeping really wasn't a better option for Ellie and us. You have to do whatever is right for your family.

17

The horror and the awe – life with a newborn

This entry is quite simply an account of Ellie's first month. When I first wrote this, I debated splitting it up and mixing the relevant entries throughout the book, but I realised as I re-read it that it actually deserves to be an entry in its own right, for several reasons:

- Firstly, because if you haven't thought about what having a newborn is like yet, then this is a great way to get started.
- Secondly, because I hope you will see many familiar things in here that will show you how absolutely normal it all is.
- Thirdly, because I really wished someone had told me some of the more practical parts of life with a newborn.
- Finally, I hope it will make you giggle.

So here we go.

Eleanor Rose was born on the 31 March. For the first two nights, Ellie had to stay on her own in the special care baby unit as she needed some extra help, whilst I stayed in the normal ward. On writing this, three observations spring to mind.

Firstly, saying 'two nights' now sounds like nothing, but at that time, it was my whole world, and it felt like a lifetime. I am sure this was partly because of being in a ward with other mums who had their babies next to them, partly because of the shock of her being so poorly, and partly because the disappointment of what had happened after a relatively straightforward birth. I also really just wanted to be at home.

Secondly, I had been totally unprepared for the sheer frustration you are likely to feel waiting to be, and being, discharged from the hospital. This is a process which truly is bureaucracy at its best. I can keenly recall my immense frustration at wanting to leave the hospital and, even more so, my absolute fury that getting Ellie and me discharged from hospital, even after it had been agreed on, was so blooming difficult.

Frustration very nearly boiled over at several points, the most memorable of which was when, finally having the paperwork done for both of us, a junior ward staff member walked past and stopped to say 'oooh, she looks a bit yellow'! Amazingly, I managed to stop myself wringing her neck and mustered a reply of 'no, she's fine, and we are going home'. Had I any doubt about her health, I wouldn't have been taking her home. Ellie had been given the all clear by the specialist, and having someone who didn't really know make such a silly comment is now quite amusing, but at that time, it was completely inappropriate.

Finally, four days after I went into hospital, we walked out with this amazing tiny baby in her car seat. My first thought was relief to be going home. My second thought, as we began to drive away, was 'oh my, we have a baby, how did this happen?'. We now had an amazing baby, I really had given birth, and this was actually real.

At this point, as a mixture of joy, relief, and sheer panic welled up inside me, I realised that I had not thought (in fact, hadn't allowed myself to think) about what life would be like after our new baby arrived. As an eternal 'planner', that was quite something. I promptly sat with tears streaming down my face as I swayed between the purest feeling of joy and absolute terror – a combination that would remain and reappear frequently over the coming months.

It was within a day of our return home from hospital that we had a realisation that Ellie is a particularly alert baby who requires not just food, warmth, sleep, and cleanliness, but entertainment (how do you entertain a newborn?!). Notably, too much of the latter caused a screaming response. I should add that I am confident in my statement of Ellie being particularly alert because a number of different health professionals specifically commented on this fact.

It is also at this time that we began to see a pattern of consistent crying starting at around 4.30 p.m. each evening and, initially, lasting until midnight or the early hours. When the initial shock wore off, we did as much research as we could and talked to friends. Thank goodness for one friend in particular who was a few weeks ahead of us and experiencing a very similar scenario. We also went for a session with my antenatal yoga teacher who specialises in helping babies with this type of issue through baby yoga. By the end of month one, there was some improvement, though life was still not the newborn sleep baby bliss I had foreseen.

At the end of the first month, Ellie's stomach pains and consistent crying usually only appeared for shorter periods each day with the use of a multitude of things (see earlier colic section). In addition, we were finally getting better (not always) at knowing what Ellie needed. We didn't have a proper full routine yet, but Ellie has a regular bedtime of 8 p.m., and having a pattern for bedtime was definitely helping her to settle down quicker, cry less at this time, and sleep better. Just like her mum, a bit of routine seemed to be comforting! Daytime snoozing is much more erratic, but regular periods of one-and-a-half-hour naps are needed. Night-time wakings are, thank the lord, now usually just twice a night.

Of particular note during this first month, was the changeover of health care which went over from my midwife to my health visitor, two very different approaches. I have to say, I struggled with my health visitor, who seemed extremely uninterested in how unsettled Ellie was because 'well, your house is tidy, so you must be OK'. Hmm. I know she was trying to be reassuring, but really, it didn't help.

The other major part of this first month was occupied with ensuring that Ellie was feeding well and putting on the weight expected of her. This is a particular focus for all new babies and more so for those, like Ellie, who don't gain weight as health visitors want them to. The dreaded percentile charts used to plot whether your babies weight gain is 'normal' in light of their birth weight are great fun for those whose babies' weights never waver. For those of us who do not have a smooth ride of the weight gain process, these charts are forever a source of stress.

Unfortunately, Ellie lost a considerable amount of weight in the first part of this month and dropped two percentiles. Fortunately, at the point where we were about to be referred, she finally began to gain. By the end of this month, Ellie was finally back to her birth weight. During this time, I consistently felt stressed about her weight and pressured in relation to breastfeeding. I particularly remember the aforementioned health visitor suggesting, after one disappointing weigh-in, that 'because Ellie isn't gaining enough weight, you might want to try topping her up'.

On asking if she was suggesting a bottle rather than breastfeeding, I was quickly told that that wasn't what was being suggested but that I should simply latch her on to feed again. To be clear, when a baby has fed enough, they will not feed any further. Ellie was not falling asleep whilst feeding nor crying after as though she was still hungry – she was simply stopping when she felt full and would then wait around three hours for her next feed.

The final key points of interest for Ellie's first month can be summed as follows:

- Day 4 – Its official, Ellie cries (lots) with tears. Apparently newborns do not usually have tears. All I can say is that Ellie did. I note this point particularly because I remember the gasp of horror from some of my friends when they saw her tears and the discussion that this was unusual. Not to me.

- Day 5 – First trip to the supermarket – very big event, and Ellie was great. She slept. Carefully lifting the car seat onto the trolley, I was given a sharp reminder by my post-labour body that I shouldn't be overdoing it. A stern look from my husband followed, and for the rest of our 'trip', I simply walked very slowly and looked.

- Day 9 – Registered Ellie's birth. A family trip out – very exciting, no, really, it was!

- Daddy went back to work – shock and horror. I can't put an exact date on this because he did an odd day or two back at work before he really went back full-time. This was a great way of easing me into it and really helped. That said, I definitely had moments of sheer panic and, as much as I can recall, several of them when he left the house in the morning. I also realise that nowhere have I yet mentioned how I would greet my husband on his arrival home from work each evening during this period. I would wait for daddy to get to the back door, where I was literally loitering with baby in arms. Upon his appearance, I would instantly plop Ellie into his arms and crawl upstairs to get away, hide, and maybe have a little snooze. Yes, it sounds awful, but I did it and not just for the first month, but for several months and even occasionally now (post-one-year-old).

- Day 13 – First proper trip out to visit a National Trust place and breastfed in public for the first time. I recall confidently saying that it wouldn't be a problem and I could feed anywhere fairly subtly (I had specifically been practising). When the time came, I realised that we had picked a glass-sided cafe in which to do it. Hmm – oh well, in for a penny, in for a pound!

- Day 13 – Ellie's cord finally fell off, so I was now discharged by the midwife (for some reason, this couldn't happen until the cord had gone). A particularly unattractive moment for Ellie and typically one which I felt the need to share with everyone: friends, family, and the odd stranger!

- Two weeks old – first baby yoga and massage class. Loved it, loved it, loved it – not only did it help Ellie's colic, but it also gave me something to do with her without having to think too much. Love it.

- At three weeks old, we had our first big day trip out and set off with huge expectations for Southwold beach. Disastrous. We got very stressed because Ellie started crying when we were just briefly looking around the beautiful, quiet church, and we couldn't work out why she was upset. Eventually, we realise that she had a dirty bum and, by that time, was overdue for a feed. Simple in hindsight, panic at the time.

One month to one year

It is a sunny day in spring 2009, and my observation is simple – my one year old daughter is amazing. My beautiful daughter is fast asleep in her pram, just inside the garage (it's cooler than the garden!), and I am drinking a well-earned cup of tea whilst I type this. Today is a good day. Ellie and I went to a music and dance group this morning, which was great fun, and we both enjoyed it (Ellie was happy after a solid night's sleep). We then came home, and Ellie ate lunch with gusto, and shortly after, she went down for her nap without a peep! Now, an hour and a half later, she is still sleeping soundly.

OK, the fact that I find this particularly noteworthy tells you this isn't how every day goes, and of course, what I haven't mentioned yet is that we have just had an absolutely hideous preceding week. It's been a combination of some 'virus' or other, teething with a vengeance, and the appearance of an oozing ear infection.

This, I feel, gives you a reasonable insight into life with a growing baby and toddler – an amazing mix of fun, laughter, hard work, and, occasionally, sheer frustration.

So to the final few entries – the seven things I wish someone had told me about having a growing baby and toddler.

18

It's a tale of three things

The more I wrote for this part of the book from the snippets I'd noted down over the months, the more I realised that the first year with my new daughter really boiled down to a constant quest to answer three key questions. These are essentially the three things that life revolved around for, by and large, an entire year!

Quite simply, I wish someone had warned me that my life would become so very intertwined with these three things and that someone had told me this was not only normal but to be expected. Maybe then, when I found myself having nothing to talk about other than these things, I wouldn't have felt quite so alien to the world.

So here, for you, is a heads-up about the three things your life will revolve around for the first year:

- Food and feeding – are they eating the right amount of the right stuff at the right time?
- Sleep – are they sleeping enough and at the right times?
- Growing – are they developing normally and growing at the right rate?

So, now you know.

19

Time flies, eventually

time flies by....

Crucially, what I notice as I finally start to write this out from my notes and scraps of paper all over the place, is that I truly cannot believe my daughter has just turned one. It has been a huge journey, both funny and frightening, and boy, oh, boy, has it gone quick! However, this is said *in retrospect,* and I have not forgotten that I got incredibly tired of people telling me 'You must enjoy every moment because the time will fly' because it didn't at the time and, actually, it wasn't all fun and games. That first year was also hard work, exhausting, and a massive, *massive* adjustment. So right now, let me be clear, this will be an incredible year, and you will no doubt remember all the funny, sweet, and amazing moments, but that really is only half the story.

The other aspect of time that I simply have to mention here is the magic of three months that is promised by all (well, most people!). The sentence shared with you by many will go something along the lines of 'It gets easier, and you'll see a huge change after three months.' I distinctly remember everyone telling me that, when you hit three months with your baby, there will be a sudden revelation, and life will become easier – colic (or whatever you want to call that incessant screaming every evening) will suddenly stop, Ellie will become calmer, and I will feel better. I, personally, was gasping for that three-month magical miracle, and not only did three months seem an awfully long time, but I have to confess that, for me, this sudden shift did not take place. For Ellie and I this was a much more gradual change, so be warned, this piece of advice might indeed be true, but it is not a guarantee.

What I can say is that, by six months, we had without doubt found ourselves in a calmer, more relaxed place, and were definitely enjoying everything more. I will also add here that for those of my friends who were blessed with happy-go-lucky, easy-going newborns, three months represented the point when they actually became much more challenging. You have been warned.

My last entry in this section has to be one final piece of time-related advice you will no doubt receive: 'You'll soon get into a routine, and it'll be easy'. This may be the case for some lucky individuals, but for others, any kind of pattern or routine may take a bit longer.

The most important thing though is to remember that getting a routine simply cannot be the end of the challenge. You have a constantly growing, changing, and developing little one, and, as such, you will constantly be challenged. At some point in the first year, it dawned on me that there is no end to the things I will need to worry about regarding my baby, toddler, and, I suspect, child and teenager later! There is simply an endless list of 'next challenges'!

20

Food, glorious food – it's a never-ending story

Now it's possible (and you may have already noticed) that I wasn't the most relaxed mother in the world and that I worried unnecessarily on many occasions. It's true that, in hindsight, I probably didn't need to worry quite so much as I did about feeding; I mean, do you know any five-years-olds who don't eat regular food? My defence, however, is that hindsight is a beautiful thing but also that people very often mislead you. Unhelpful advice, comments, and conversations have been featured in several places throughout this book, and here is yet another one.

It's commonly said that the move from milk to solids enables your baby not only to sleep better and be more content, but it also stops you having to worry about their feeding. The first part of this is simply not necessarily true, but more importantly, the second part is definitely not true. The move to solids does not represent a huge watershed moment of no longer needing to think about or indeed worry about feeding – it just means you think about other aspects of feeding. The journey will vary for everyone, but forewarned is forearmed, so here, for your consideration, is a very quick run-through of the stages associated with feeding and the associated concerns that are likely to come up:

- Stage 1: The milk intake – How many ounces are they having? How many feeds? Is it enough, and are they growing enough?

- Stage 2: Increasing daytime intake and decreasing night-time intake so as to facilitate sleep – Which feeds do I decrease in the daytime? How do I stretch them between feeds? When do I finally drop the 10 to 10.30 p.m. feed?

- Stage 3: The move to solids – How do I get them to eat *solids (aka purees)*? What should the first solid be? When should I try it, that is, what week, what day, and what time? How much should they eat? How quickly should I add in new foods? Ahhhhh, they are sick! Why?

As a slight side note here – please don't be fooled into thinking that once your little angel settles having 'solids' it's onwards and upwards. They trick you that way, but actually, they will frequently go backwards with their tastes and their volumes.

- Stage 4: Establishing mealtimes and reducing milk – Growing babies need growing nutrients, so gradually, milk must be replaced by solids. How do I reduce milk? When should I? How on earth do I get them to wait for meal times when they've previously been fed in some way every few hours!?

- Stage 5: Progressing solids – You begin to focus on moving them to thicker purees, finger food, and then lumpy food (or whatever order you go in). I note that some schools of thought advise that your baby starts on finger food from day one – I've no idea if this prevents this particular stage of worry as I have no experience from which to draw. The concerns here are, then, when to progress, in what order, and how.

- Stage 6: Separate meals – At some point, you eventually ask yourself how you ended up making totally separate meals for you and your child and make a move to combining the two.

My usual disclaimer applies here; this is not written as a guide to stages of weaning, but the point here is that you won't suddenly stop thinking about food or feeding at any stage in this first year. This is normal.

Before we move on, I must give a little reminder once again that parenting is not for the squeamish as clearly you will not only be concerned with what's going in but also with what's coming out. Are they pooping sufficiently, and does it look right? You really will review their poo and, in all likelihood, discuss it with several people on a regular basis. I recall being given pictures of baby poo at my NCT class and thinking it was all a little odd; however, weeks later, I found myself comparing the picture to my daughter's poo. Need I say more?

So to my final point on this particular topic – feeding is messy, really messy. For one thing, bibs are all designed with one fault; they cannot stop your child from getting messy. Hands regularly get in the way as, occasionally, do toes, and the wonderful raspberry noise that you encouraged is now your worst enemy. Floor mats, bibs, muslin cloths – none of these will change the fact that it is messy. In the end, Ellie ate where there were no carpets, no walls within reach, and ideally for her, no clothes on. Fabulous.

21

'Sleeping through the night' can mean different things – no, really!

This particular entry has justified its own unique place in the list of twenty-four purely because of the potentially high impact it has.

You and everyone else will be obsessed with how quickly your baby sleeps through the night. It's worth noting, however, that different people define 'through the night' in different ways. I know it sounds crazy. I recall when I first had this revelation – I was almost speechless with the absurdity of it. Let me explain.

For some, a four-hour stint with no waking up is in their view 'sleeping through the night'. For others, it's if they go to bed at 11 p.m. and don't wake until 7 a.m. For me, 'through the night' really means from 7 or 8 p.m. until 6 or 7 a.m. at the earliest! So when I heard so many others were sleeping through the night and my little one wasn't, I have to be honest and say, I was very worried and felt really miserable. That was, until I got to the bottom of what 'through the night' really meant.

So save yourself the same worry, and when the moment arrives that another mummy says 'oh, are they not sleeping through yet? My daisy is', just remember . . . gloating like that deserves a question or two.

22

Health professionals will be your new best friends

Ellie unfortunately got an infected belly button towards the end of the first month, and this was my not-so-smooth introduction to the fact that I would now see my doctor, health visitor, and accident and emergency service more than I had in my entire pre-baby life – all thirty-one years.

No, I am not exaggerating. Here is just a brief rundown of Ellie's first year in terms of her health or, more accurately, illness:

Month two:

- Ellie's belly button has been oozing, so we went to the see the health visitor. Promptly advised to see the GP. Swab taken and given some antibiotic cream.

- Belly button not clearing up, so return trip to GP. GP cauterised the wound to heal it.

- Six week check at GP. Checked hips, eyes, belly button, and heart. Changed cream for belly button as swab showed anaerobic infection and needs different treatment.

- First immunisations and belly button check again. Belly button needed to be cauterised for the second time.

Month three:

- Hospital visit for Ellie's follow-up hip scan – all clear, so signed off.

- Second Immunisations at doctors – lovely.

Months four and five:

- Third set of immunisations – three this time. Ellie not impressed but calmed within a second of leaving the surgery.

- Ellie has got mild gastroenteritis – confirmed by GP. She is very poorly and has diarrhoea, which has caused horrendous nappy rash. Saw the GP twice – advised to give Calpol and Nurofen whilst continuing to put cream on for the nappy rash. GP recommends fresh air on her bum for the nappy rash and bed mats all over the floor so her diarrhoea doesn't get on anything. Joy.

- Nappy rash remains well after the gastroenteritis has gone, with Ellie's bum red raw. This takes several weeks to clear.

Month six:

- Ellie has her first cold – massaged Snufflebabe vapour rub into her chest and toes. Calpol to reduce her distress in the night.

Month seven:

- Ellie has another cold – bad.

- Pre-first-year check-up at clinic with health visitor. All fine.

Month ten:

- Ellie appears to have some sort of viral infection which came on in the night. Up every two hours with a cry. Generally unhappy, high temp (38.9°C highest), and crying a lot. Needs holding by Mummy – Calpol *and* Nurofen.

- Seven days later, Ellie is finally showing signs of getting better – her temperature is finally coming under control without double doses of medication. At its worst, her temp hit 40.3°C. Have been to the GP twice and to the doctors on call on Saturday. In addition to the snotty nose, bad temper, and high temperature, Ellie also has *very* waxy ears and horrid brown stuff coming out of her nose.

- Nine days on, we took Ellie to emergency doctors on call at Ipswich because her ear is now clearly oozing gunk and bothering her. Confirmed that it is an ear infection – despite having been told, when specifically asking twice, that it wasn't (GP and emergency clinic). Given antibiotics and told to get to GP by Wednesday.

- Trip to the GP as advised. Given new prescription of ear drops.

- A further six days later, I took Ellie to the doctors *again*. Ear infection is just not getting any better. Advised to stop ear drops GP originally gave and to change the antibiotic as it's clearly not working. Given alternative antibiotics and a swab of ear taken.

- A month after the original infection, we go back to the doctors yet again – given a third lot of antibiotics.

- Almost a month later, back to the GP as Ellie's ear is still not right – still oozing. Given yet more antibiotics and an explanation given that this has now been two different infections. Ellie has now also developed a cough.

- Finally, five days after the last appointment, Ellie seems better for the first time since this started. Her ear is no longer oozing, and her cough is almost gone. One final check-up with the doctor to confirm the infection has actually gone this time.

- Ellie had her twelve-month immunisation. One injection only and she recovered from it *very* quickly, with a rice cake.

Now the above does not include the regular weigh-ins and checks with the health visitor at the clinic nor does it have anything to do with my health. So, hopefully, this gives you a flavour for how familiar you are likely to become with health services and health professionals.

The point of including this is as a heads-up and reassurance that this is what happens. It is, of course, different for different people, but the theme of seeing health professionals a lot is definitely a common thread between all parents of new babies and toddlers.

23

Plan your next baby now – or prepare your answer!

I recall the health visitor talking to me on our first appointment after I got out of hospital about having sex again and reminding me that we needed to be careful as it's possible to conceive another baby straight away – unless, she added, we wanted to. As I guffawed quite loudly, I then realised that she wasn't kidding. Not only did she think I wanted to have sex again anytime soon and would be able to, she also thought that by some miracle I might have the time and energy. Not to mention that she thought I, with a very new baby, might have the inclination to have another!

I remember feeling completely and utterly incredulous at the whole conversation. At the later point of being discharged by the health visitor and left with a 'see you when you have your next one', I finally decided that she was lovely . . . but clearly quite mad. I soon discovered, however, that the whole world had gone slightly mad when, suddenly, person after person (family, friend, and complete strangers) started to ask *that* question: So, when are you having your next one?

In fact, many felt this was a good question to ask when my daughter was just a couple of months old! Most annoying is that they actually asked 'when' not 'if'. Whether or not at any point in the future having more children is on the cards is yet to be decided – right then, I had an amazing, beautiful, special little girl who needed and deserved all my time.

What I truly wished every time was that I wouldn't feel quite so shocked about the question and that I had some incredibly witty and tart remark ready to fire back. Sadly, I never did. So here's your chance to get ahead of the game and think about how you're going to reply to that question. The best answer I've heard so far is to look pensively at the baby and say in a thoughtful voice 'I've not decided if I'm keeping this one yet'.

24

Don't forget about you

The placement of this final entry is not an indication that it's of least importance, but in fact, it's the opposite. This is my final entry because you simply have to remember it.

In all the excitement, amazement, madness, and emotion of the first year as a new parent, do not forget about you. Everyone, from almost day one, went on about making sure I got time for me. The fact is that this is easier said than done, so the point of this entry is to get you to prioritise yourself properly and give some pointers of how you might do this in practice.

My top tips are simple:

- Find one easy thing that you can do that makes you feel good. Have a bath, go for a walk, watch a favourite TV programme, or do your nails. Find it, and do it . . . regularly.

- Really do make use of friends and family who offer to babysit – it's a hard thing to do, but do it. Use the time to have a meal out with your partner or see friends. Most importantly, use the time to be you, the grown-up, adult you. (This piece of advice is given from a 'do as I say, not as I did' perspective – but I know I got this wrong.)

And so . . .

. . . there it is, all the things that I'd wished someone had told me about pregnancy, birth, and the first eighteen months, written down for you.

I hope you've enjoyed reading it, and I hope that you've found it useful.

As I finally finish this book, my little girl has turned four and is due to start school soon. The funny thing is that since she was two, I really haven't felt the same drive to write things down, but suddenly, as we start to enter the world of school, I'm finding a new plethora of things that just might be good to share.

See you soon!

Sharon

Author Biography

Sharon Smyth is a working mum and author based in the United Kingdom. Sharon graduated from Loughborough University and pursued a career in human resources. Becoming a mum at 31 Sharon found herself driven to share her experiences with others on the same journey and used her practical, down to earth style to write her first book 'The things they never tell you about becoming mum'. Sharon enjoys reading, spending time with family and friends, writing her blog and being constantly surprised by her daughter.

You can find out more from her website:

www.sharonsmyth.co.uk

Index

A

advice   13-14, 43, 94
  on baby care and
    breastfeeding   44-5
  on colicky babies   60, 79
  on itchy bellies   25
  sharing a room   67-8
  unhelpful   53-4, 81
Anger   51
antenatal classes   23, 44, 71

B

babies:
  colicky   58
  comparing   56, 67
  first year of   77, 79-80, 83
  newborn *see* newborns
  sleep of   55
belly, itchy   25
birth plan   15, 27-9, 91
bottle feeding   62-3, 72
breastfeeding   45-8, 51, 54, 62-3

C

caesarean births   19
calamine lotion   25-6
Calpol   88-9
colic   58-60, 66, 79
comparisons *see* babies,
    comparing
contractions   32, 35, 37
conversations, unhelpful *see*
    zoning out
cord *see* umbilical cord

D

delivery   29, 34-8
depression, post-natal   50
dummy   63-5

E

Eleanor Rose *see* Ellie (daughter)
Ellie (daughter):
  belly button infection of   87-8

99

Printed in Great Britain
by Amazon